THESE STRATEGIES WILL IMPROVE YOUR LIFE

I'm sure you already know that serious emotional pain is very real, and has reached epidemic proportions around the world. What you may not know, is that most of this suffering is completely avoidable. Please suspend disbelief for just a couple of minutes so you can read what other people have to say about the strategies that you are about to learn.

The information that you are about to learn (and apply) had such an emormous impact on one of our readers that he agreed it was important to openly share his unsolicited letter:

"I wanted to tell you a little about myself and my story. I'll keep it brief, as the details are numerous. But to shorten a longer story, I'm recently coming out of a toxic marriage of almost 9 years. My wife left in early January and I had been having a very rough time accepting the reality of my situation. On March 6th, I attempted suicide. I severed my brachial artery and nearly bled out. A few family members, with the help of the police, were able to find me and save my life. I spent the next two weeks in a psych hospital, during which time I was given your book "Think Yourself Happy".

When I got the book, I didn't think much of it. I was very depressed and not sure if I wanted to keep going. On top of that, I'm not much of a reader anyhow.

So at first, I had very little intention of even reading the book. But one evening... as I read through the book, the words sunk in deeply. And each time I pick-

ed the book up again, it swept over me like an ocean wave, cresting into waves of hope. I thought about everything going on in my life and came to see everything from an entirely new perspective.

The worry in my heart began to vanish, as it was weighed out by a new confidence that I never had. I've spent a lot of my life in the "poor me" way of thinking, and your book allowed me to think from a new place and take control of myself and my happiness.

I do not know the words to describe how grateful I am for your book. Perhaps it was the timing in my life in which I received the book, but I feel consumed by it's message. For the first time in many years, I feel inspired, hopeful, and in control. I enjoyed that the book was fairly short, and straight to the point, because larger books tend to overwhelm me and I'd have otherwise probably not even began reading it. But instead, I've actually read it twice! (The only book I've ever read twice).

I'm writing to express my gratitude for your contribution to the world. I'm sure this book has had a similar effect on many who have read it and I just wanted to say that I am extremely thankful for your book. It has literally saved my life.

While I was in the psychiatric hospital after my suicide attempt, I met quite a few other people who were in a similar place I was in, whom I now call friends. They were hopeless, depressed, and just down and out. I thought of your book and wanted to help them see the world in a new way as I have, and I wanted to hand out copies to nearly everyone there, but I have *nowhere near the kind of funds to do that. I even told the psychiatrist at the hospital that I think at least one copy of the book should be kept in each dorm room in the hospital for people to read, although she was fairly unresponsive to the request.*

But I have been unequivocally inspired by your book. And I want to give that hope and perspective to others who are in dire need of a sense of direction and control over their lives. I know quite a few people who would benefit greatly from your book, and I would love to be able to spread the message to those who need it. Ever since I read your book, I have wanted to give this gift of inner peace to others, and I feel a strong feeling within me that I must. That I am destined to it.

A friend of mine who I visited this past Saturday has been in a really bad place for a long time. He is an army veteran who suffers from PTSD and depression. When I walked into his room, he was sitting in the dark, upright in a chair, with his head in his lap. Just sitting there. His roommates told me he's been doing that a lot lately, and I felt so overwhelmed with sadness for him.

After I got him talking he brightened up fairly quick-ly and we had a pretty fun night. But what I realized that night... is that I have the ability to help people. And I feel like that realization has stricken me in the most profound of ways, and I feel like I gained a new purpose in life. I want to help people who are in the position I was in.

I wanted to see if you would be willing to send me

some free copies of your book to hand out. I have quite a few individual friends that I believe could greatly benefit from your book, and I would like to donate several copies to the psych hospitals around central Ohio to give those in need an opportunity to change their way of thinking, and take control of their happiness!

As I close this letter, I feel a sense of pride and some shame. I'm not one to comfortably ask for handouts, but I can't afford to purchase copies of the book for all those I'd like to give it to, and if I could get maybe 10-20 copies, I ensure you I would make good use of them!!"

Sincerely,

— Jeremy, Central Ohio

This is not an isolated occurance. This is just one example of the many people who are in desperate need of these skills, tools, and action strategies to live a happy and successful life.

If you know a person who needs this information now, please send them to:

www.ThinkYourselfHappy.com

What Influencers Are Saying About Think Yourself Happy

"I want to encourage you to get this book. Why? If you don't program yourself, you will be programmed. And so this book is about taking charge of your mind, being not conformed to this world, being transformed by the renewing of your mind. Think Yourself Happy helps you to do that each and every day. So make sure you get it now. Make it important. Make it a priority because it will literally transform your life!"
— **Les Brown,** World's #1 Motivational Speaker, Former Congressman, and Bestselling Author

"Sometimes, it's the simplest things that can make the biggest difference in our lives. Think Yourself Happy is a great little read to help you learn how to achieve happiness."
— **Tom Hopkins,** author, The Official Guide to Success and When Buyers Say No

"Think Yourself Happy is such a powerful testament to how we can control our own happiness by training ourselves to think happily, not just in the moment, but to change our thought processes to find the clarity to pursue that which truly drives you. Greg Jacobson's clear, positive writing not only inspires the reader to want to make these changes, but breaks them down into easily understood components that removes the barriers we set up to making these changes. Think Yourself Happy should be on everyone's reading list."
— **Keith Ferrazzi,** Author of Two #1 NY Times Bestsellers Who's Got Your Back & Never Eat Alone

"Greg Jacobson has done a masterful job of outlining specific, actionable tools to allow people to create happiness regardless of circumstances."
— **Darren Kavinoky,** Celebrity Legal Analyst, Top Trial Lawyer & TV Host

"When you learn the principles in this book, your entire life will change. He is a great mentor!"
— **Forbes Riley,** Sold Over $2½ Billion in Products on TV

"Clear. Attainable. Indispensable."
— **Joseph McClendon III,** Neuropsychologist, Peak Performance Expert and Best-Selling Author of Get Happy Now!

"...what truly constitutes happiness, with simple but profound steps to achieve and sustain it while focusing on the greater good. A must read for every busy person. It will transform your thinking... And your life!"
— **Dr. Betty Uribe,** Senior VP California Bank & Trust

"Greg has an amazing way of empowering people to take immediate action and achieve extraordinary results."
— **Jason Gary,** Award-Winning Cinematographer

"I loved the brilliant simplicity of this book. Rooted in science, it still offers everyday wisdom. From now on, all of my obstacles will be considered opportunities!"
— **John Burke,** 3-Time Emmy Award-Winning Host & Actor

"Happiness is not a random occurrence. The foundations necessary to make happiness your daily experience are found in this book."
— **Bob Kaehler,** Three-Time Olympian and Four-Time World Champion Rower

"Greg Jacobson's content is clear, concise, and powerful."
— **Alex Tuira,** CEO of Ngakau Aroha Investments Ltd.

"Happy people, equals happy business! Greg Jacobson shows you how to make it even better."
— **Jeffrey Hayzlett,** Primetime TV & Podcast Host and Chairman of C-Suite Network

"Read the book!"
— **Michael E. Gerber,** Worlds #1 Small Business Guru - Inc. Magazine, New York Times Bestselling Author of "The E-Myth" Series

"Preparation and hard work are critical, it starts with mental preparation and Greg Jacobson makes the process easy."
— **Coach Lou Holtz,** Former NFL Head Coach, College Football Hall of Fame Legend, TV Sports Analyst

"This is a great book that shows you how to be happy – starting immediately."
— **Brian Tracy,** New York Times Bestselling Author, Speaker, Consultant

THINK
YOURSELF
HAPPY

Five Changes In Thinking
That Will Immediately
Improve Your Life

GREG JACOBSON

Before You Get Started

Find Out Your Score:
www.TheHappinessQuiz.com

_894_
_____
YOUR HAPPINESS SCORE

© January 2020 Third Printing

ISBN# 978-0-9973319-4-3

Printed in the USA

Archer-Gimbal Publishing

For Rocky, Tanner, Dillon, and Austin...
I love you, and I'm proud of you!

Contents

0 Introduction   1

1 Why Be Happy?   9

2 It's All In Your Head   23

3 The Five Changes To Think Yourself Happy   33

4 Change #1: **Visualization**   41

5 Change #2: **Positive Anticipation**   51

6 Change #3: **Meaning**   59

7 Change #4: **Perspective**   67

8 Change #5: **Gratitude**   75

9 Conclusion: The Science Of Happily Achieving   83

10 Acknowledgments   93

11 About Greg Jacobson   97

12 Positive Psychology Research   101

13 Notes   105

0
INTRODUCTION

"You can't hire someone else
to do your push-ups for you."
— **Jim Rohn**

In 1988, I was about to turn 20. The Internet was an infant, cell phones looked like giant bricks, and there were no laptops, flat screens, or satellite TV. My parents were divorced and I was living with my mom and her new husband in Tarzana, California — a middle-class suburb near Los Angeles. Not much was happening in my life at the time, so I hung around on their couch watching TV.

That same year, the US government lifted the regulations governing commercial content on TV, removing the restriction on commercials being a maximum of 18 minutes in length. *Kaboom!* Infomercials burst onto TV sets everywhere and the sales pitches were amazing!

This new way of marketing to the masses exploded with detailed offers promising secrets to real-estate investing, miracle health cures, and amazing personal development. But for infomercials to be effective, advertisers needed *a lot* of time, and they needed to buy that time for as little as possible.

Television stations make money by selling advertising. If they don't sell every spot available, that time gets filled either by giving top-paying advertisers extra commercial time, or by selling it at a discount. These spots, known as remnants, are perfect for infomercial product marketing — cheap time, and lots of it. Remnants are generally offered late at night or early in the morning in the hours when most people aren't watching TV.

Luckily for me, I *was* watching. And amidst the 'get rich quick' pitches, promises of miracle hair growth, and devices to cut housework in half, one offer stood out from all the rest — literally. A giant of a man, standing every bit of 6'7" tall with unstoppable confidence and energy pouring out of him like the sun, had a powerful message that seriously spoke to me. I was mesmerized. The more I watched this guy, the more he made sense and the more of what he said resonated with me. Although I'd read dozens of books on success, seeing others using a system I could follow step-by-step was a new option that I felt would work for me.

My birthday was coming up and I told my mom the gift I wanted more than anything else was *Personal Power*, a 30-day cassette program for creating a better life. My mom was shocked. "That's what you want?" she asked. I told her, "Once I learn the secrets this guy, Tony Robbins, is teaching, we can all have everything we ever want. It is only going to be a $195 investment, an excellent value. Also, with my new motivation and the skill-sets I'm about to learn, I'll be able to move out soon." My mom, who's always been one of my greatest supporters, bought me those tapes without hesitation. (Mom, you rock!) I listened to the entire 30-day program over the next 48 hours and then started them over again and again until I got the message loud and clear. **The message was:**

IF IT'S TO BE, IT'S UP TO ME.

Nothing was going to happen for me in a big way unless I made it happen. There's only one shortcut I know, I could follow others who'd achieved the results I was looking for and do what they did. However, I didn't know anybody personally that fit those descriptions.

But I got started anyway. It all starts with getting started. These ideas, strategies, and tools come from more than 35 years of reading hundreds of books, listening to thousands of hours of cassettes, CDs & mp3s, watching and attending hundreds of seminars, and listening to thousands of interviews. I've been researching and studying the masters of every area of life that's important to me, applying these methods, strategies, and paradigms in my own life with great success, and then teaching others. I speak internationally, mentor, consult, and show people how to live a better quality of life.

With no startup money, we bought concert and sporting event tickets on credit cards that we borrowed from everyone we knew, then sold the tickets and paid them back with interest. We did this every week. This process grew to a business that generated over $30,000,000 annually in net profits. It took 5 years of 100+ hour work weeks without a day off to build it, but we did although there was no time to enjoy it.

Then I had an epiphany that changed everything. I went from working 100-hour, crazy-productive work-weeks to taking a 10-year sabbatical, spending priceless time with my family, traveling around the world several times, and learning there's a lot more I want to learn.

My focus went from helping myself and the people in my inner circle, to understanding that everyone and everything on this planet is important. Contributing to making this world, and the people on it, better is what I do every day.

Helping people achieve ultra-high levels of success in any (and all) areas of their lives is my area of expertise, but more than that, I've become a specialist in helping people **Happily Achieve**.

When high achievers are successful, but unfulfilled, they call me. We work through the difficult areas of their life and I help them get clarity, and to the point where they can be happy <u>and</u> successful. You may not think those two feelings are separate, but they often are.

Success, for many people, equals stress, fear, strained relationships, poor health, and a lot of other negative consequences. But in truth, it's easier to be successful and achieve your goals **while** you're happy. That's what I teach. And I believe that's the reason you're reading this book.

I'm here to help you learn how to **Think Yourself Happy.** It's not complicated, but you'll have to make five changes in the way you think. To get results, you must take action and invest the time and energy necessary to learn a few specific skills that will reshape your thoughts and emotions.

The entire process takes only a few minutes a day, and soon you'll find yourself thinking in new and different ways — ways that'll help you be happy no matter what your external circumstances are.

Are you willing to do whatever it takes to make your life spectacular?

People who achieve excellence at anything got there by disciplined, scheduled practice — not willpower. I'll deliver for you, but you need to jump in at some point and do the exercises. If you don't like how the word 'exercises' makes you feel, look at it as an opportunity to create a better quality of life, but you are still required to take action.

Look, you can do what you normally do, but then you'll only get the results you normally get. That isn't why you're reading this book. If you want real results, you need to commit to doing something different than what you've been doing so far.

Small changes over time yield great results. Adopting even one of these five changes in your thinking will help you be happier every day.

And when you're happier, life feels better. Your relationships are easier. Work becomes less of a challenge, even a joy, rather than a chore.

You'll find yourself Happily Achieving more than you ever believed possible, simply by changing a few habits of thought.

Are You Ready? Let's Get Started.

1
WHY BE HAPPY?

*"Success is not the key to happiness,
happiness is the key to success."*
— **Albert Schweitzer**

Could you be happier than you are right now? Is there anything you can do to actively increase your level of happiness? If there are things you can do to make yourself happier, why wouldn't you do them?

According to Joseph McClendon III in his book, Get Happy Now, only an estimated 3.5 percent of people are happy, positive, and optimistic.[1]

In 2013, The US ranked 17th on the World Happiness Report trailing such 'under developed' countries as Mexico, Panama, and Costa Rica.[2]

This lack of happiness is showing up as different kinds of psychological problems. Studies show that in the US, 20 percent of people will suffer from a mood disorder sometime in their lives, 30 percent from an anxiety disorder, and about 9 percent from depression. Currently, around 25 percent of women and 5 percent of men are on some kind of antidepressant, and almost 50 percent of both men and women admit to using food to improve their mood.[3]

Bottom line? Far too many of us aren't very good at being happy.

And despite medications, counseling, food, and other distractions, our happiness level remains stubbornly low, and decreasing at an alarming rate.

We need to fix this NOW. Not simply because it's just better to be happy with yourself, but because there is an entire body of research in positive psychology that shows how important happiness is in every area of your life.

People Who Are Happy...

- Earn more money
- Learn faster and easier
- Live longer
- Are more productive
- Are better and faster problem solvers
- Have improved health
- Contribute more
- Are more creative
- Have stronger, longer lasting relationships
- Have a more positive attitude
- Make fewer mistakes
- Are married longer
- Have lower divorce rates
- Are more enjoyable to be around
- Are better team players
- Report greater life satisfaction[4]

What Do You Need To Be Happy?

I've observed two obstacles that get in the way of people experiencing happiness on a regular basis. The first is what I call the 'then I'll' problem.

For Example...

- ⬧ Once I get the promotion, then I'll be happy.

- ⬧ If he/she goes out with me, then I'll be happy.

- ⬧ If I pass this test, then I'll be happy.

- ⬧ When I come in first, then I'll be happy.

- ⬧ When my kid graduates, then I'll be happy.

- ⬧ When I become rich, then I'll be happy.

- ⬧ When I pay off my debts, then I'll be happy.

- ⬧ When I get that promotion, then I'll be happy.

- ⬧ When I retire, then I'll be happy.

- ⬧ When I lose the weight, then I'll be happy.

- ⬧ When I have grandkids, then I'll be happy.

Most of us were taught that happiness would come after we earned it. By listening to our parents and teachers, studying hard in school, getting into a great university, landing a fantastic job, finding the perfect mate, having a challenge-free relationship, working hard and earning promotions along the way, following along, not breaking the rules or rocking the boat, possibly having some flawless kids... If you do all that, then happiness will be there waiting for you at the end of it all.

That game sounds rigged, and not in your favor. With this kind of thinking, you'll spend your life waiting and wanting to be happy, but never giving yourself the chance to **feel happy in the moment.** And that's all there is — right here, right now.

When you think you have to reach a milestone or attain a goal in order to be happy, you're trading one moment of happiness for days, weeks, months, and even years of unrewarded effort at best, and active unhappiness at worst.

I believe happiness isn't something you have to earn; it's something you already deserve. **Everyone deserves to be happy — and everyone has that opportunity any day, any moment, anytime. You just have to learn how, and then do it.**

The second obstacle to happiness is 'more.' Here's the story of how I screwed that up.

In 1999, I was the founder and principal partner of what would become the largest wholesale ticket company in the world. By 2007, Wiseguy Tickets would be buying over a million concert, sports, and theater tickets a year and supplying North America's largest brokers with the tickets they'd resell to the public.

My business partner, Ken, and I had known and worked with each other since we were 16 years old. Both of us ran a 'crew' of junior high school students, driving them to different neighborhoods to sell newspaper subscriptions door-to-door for the Daily News. We'd each train our own kids and then have them recruit their friends. It was fun and we were very good at it and highly competitive.

I started Wiseguy after years of working for a large entertainment magazine selling advertising. I was strongly positioned to meet lots of amazing, talented, connected people. I learned a lot by just watching and listening. But when I finally decided to walk away from a solid, steady paycheck and give everything to building the wholesale ticket business, Ken and I were both truly **all in**. Day and night, whenever there was enough energy to work, we worked. We put our blood and sweat into building this business to provide everything we could for our families.

We wanted to give them the luxury lifestyles we longed for, but didn't have as kids.

We worked hard at being smarter and asking better questions than our competition. Averaging 110–120 hours a week for years straight without a vacation, we designed and built a real money machine.

We sacrificed precious time **with** our families so we could buy more **for** them. It made us feel like heavy hitters while allowing them to feel privileged and lucky. But we were always working.

Within a couple of years, the value of our company was well in excess of $250,000,000 and going up quickly. In fact, 'excess' would be the company's mantra. But this trajectory eventually took Ken and I in very different directions.

On December 30, 1999, we were finally enjoying our first well-deserved, first-class vacation alone with our wives since we started Wiseguy Tickets.

My sons, Tanner, Dillon, and Austin, were staying with my dad and his wife for a few weeks. We were committed to doing this vacation right.

For our first ten days, we rented a private villa in Bali, Indonesia, overlooking a jungle canyon and the river below.

This night, however, we were celebrating at the exquisite Amandari Resort.

It was Lina's birthday, Ken's wife. As luck would have it, Rocky (my wife) had a friend who happened to be the new head chef of this six-star resort and arranged for us to experience a private chef's creation dinner just for us.

When we arrived, we were led through a garden area then across a bridge to our table, which sat alone on a small island in the middle of a secluded, private lake under a beautifully lit palapa (a thatched-roof pavilion). It was spectacular. It felt like everything we'd ever dreamed about had come true. All of those long hours of work for so many years had allowed us to create this incredible experience.

During a break between courses, Ken wanted to smoke a cigar (he was really into that), so we left the girls and went for a short walk.

We walked around the simple yet stunning resort for a few minutes before stopping by another pond where dozens of very large koi swam over to visit us, thinking that we must have food for them.

I asked Ken, "What's it going to take to have more of this?" My thinking was along the lines of "How can we spend less time working and invest more time enjoying our lives?"

But the answer he came up with wasn't in line with what I was thinking at all. He said, "More! We need more of everything. We need more money, more power, more domination!"

I remember thinking, *Who is this guy, and how'd we end up thinking so differently?* I just shook my head because I knew my life's purpose was certainly not to amass more — and his was. I just wanted to slow down. I didn't want to trade more money for less time.

That moment kicked me into changing everything about my life and business. I realized my priorities had been out of line with what was most important to me — what truly made me happy. Work was getting all of my energy, time, and attention instead of it going to the people I care about most.

At the end of January 2000, I arranged to sell my half of the business.

By the end of that year, I'd abdicated all corporate responsibilities and walked away from that business forever. Life for me changed in a big way.

My focus and energy went from being a successful business operator, to working on being an excellent husband, dad, friend, and person. I grew creatively, spiritually, and altruistically. I practiced and learned to be fully present in the moment — right now. And I found I was a lot happier out of the trap of pursuing more. Going further, I've learned to appreciate the value of simplicity; equating to more freedom and less stress.

When you obsess about wanting more than you currently have or have achieved, you lose the joy of experiencing what's right here, happening right now.

Have you ever heard someone who's materially successful today reminiscing nostalgically about their earlier days, when they lived in a tiny apartment and ate dinner off of a coffee table in front of the TV, delighted that they could afford a take-out meal instead of a frozen one?

Or have you ever been around someone whom you think has a great significant other, but they can't seem to appreciate him or her because they're fantasizing about their 'ideal' soul mate instead of putting effort and energy into making the relationship they already have more ideal?

Our culture in the US is driven by ambition and aspirations, and always looking for the next level, but if ambition and aspiration stops us from being happy with what we have now, then we're missing what life's all about. Life is your memory of the moments you've experienced. You can be happy and achieve without losing your edge.

I believe it's possible to be both happy and ambitious. That's the drive of my life and what I teach others. It's not complicated, you simply have to change the way you think. Luckily, that's a lot easier than most of us believe.

What Does Happiness Look Like?

Think of the last time you were happy. You woke up on the right side of the bed, or you and your spouse or your kids were getting along particularly well.

It could be you felt your team had done a particularly good job on a project, or you handled a customer service issue gracefully and the customer said,

"Thank you," and you felt appreciated. Maybe you did something kind for someone and you felt good about yourself.

Can you think of such a time? (If not, you really need this book.) How would you describe your happiness at that moment?

Most of us think of happiness as an emotion, and it is — to some extent. But the kind of happiness I think is most valuable is a 'mood' or 'state of mind' of being happy. It's more sustainable than an emotion; you can be in a happy mood or state of mind for much longer than you can feel the elation of the emotion called 'happiness'. Happiness shouldn't be misunderstood for pleasure.

Altought pleasure is one from of happiness, it lives in the shallowest end of the happy pool. Pleasure is a sensation or momenty satisfaction of a craving. It's like scratching an itch or eating a big meal when you're hungry, even sexual gratification; it feels great, but it never lasts long enough.

Also, there is never an inappropriate time to be happy. Pleasure is not always appropriate in every situation.

I believe the mood or state of mind of happiness is fundamentally unselfish. Yes, you're the one feeling it, but usually it occurs because you're involved with something more than just yourself. In studying happiness, I've found that it must be benefit the greater good, or it's unsustainable and short-lived.

All of us have the desire to feel these kinds of happy moods and states of mind. In fact, I think most people would *love* to live a happier life.

They want to be able, not necessarily to whistle as they skip down the street, but to feel that kind of effortless satisfation, ease, and optimism as their usual state of being.

People need to have access to happiness without having to achieve anything to deserve it, but how do we learn to do that? It goes agaisnt everything we've been taught about happiness... that it comes only with accomplishments.

Unfortunately, you can't *will* yourself to be happy. However, there are specific steps you can take to *become significantly happier*. By implementing these scientifically provens method, you can attain and maintain higher levels of happiness and life satisfaction in just minutes a day.

It's time to set yourself up to win every step of the way. It starts by understanding the power of your thoughts.

Chapter Summary

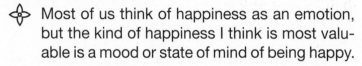

- Most of us think of happiness as an emotion, but the kind of happiness I think is most valuable is a mood or state of mind of being happy.

- Happiness shouldn't be misunderstood for pleasure. Pleasure is a sensation or momentary satisfaction of a craving. It feels good for a little while, never lasts long, and isn't always appropriate.

- The mood or state of mind of happiness is fundamentally unselfish; it usually occurs because you're involved with something more than just yourself.

- You can't will yourself to be happy, however there are some specific steps you can take to become happier.

WHAT TO DO NEXT:

<u>**WATCH THIS VIDEO**</u>

- www.ThinkYourselfHappy.com/Chapter-1

2
It's All In Your Head

*"The happiness of your life
depends upon the quality of your thoughts."*
— **Marcus Aurelius**

Since I'm committed to constant self-improvement, I regularly attend seminars to learn new skills and systems. One such event was held over several consecutive days in Santa Barbara, California. There were about a hundred of us in the class. The facilitators put us into pairs and led us through a series of questions and some interesting exercises.

Being open to new processes, both Rocky and I were committed to doing all the exercises without prejudging. Even though some of the exercises felt unnecessarily uncomfortable to me, I still participated fully.

On the second night of the seminar, our homework was to fill in the blank in this phrase: "Life is _____."

To me, this was easy, because at this point in my life, things matter. Every minute matters and I'm purposefully crafting, designing, and really living life happily every single day.

Now, I know that living with purpose probably isn't the normal way most people live, but I thought my answer to this question about what life is couldn't be too far off normal, right?

Morning came, and as I learned from one of my mentors, with a new seat comes a new perspective, so I sat in a different seat, this time, in the center of the back row.

The facilitator asked for the hands of the people

who'd done their homework and nearly everyone raised their hand.

He said, "So let me ask you, what is life? I'd like to hear your answers."

My hand shot up with about 60 others and the facilitator started calling on people.

He pointed and someone yelled out, "Pain!"

"Disappointment," said the next girl.

Then he pointed to me. I yelled, "Life is f*cking awesome!" I meant it — I wasn't trying to be the funny guy. It was totally heartfelt and genuine.

The facilitator's response was, "Too broad." And he moved on.

A woman in her forties added, "Life is heartbreak." A teenager mumbled, "Sadness." Then a guy said, "Waiting to die."

Wait, what? Hold on here... Life is waiting to die? Who are the people in this room? Are all these people (who are clearly hurting inside) an accurate representation of how the average person in this world feels?

My heart sank. I was feeling grateful and lucky for how amazing my life is in every area with so many people around me in sadness. I didn't realize the pain most people are living in — not at all.

The facilitator said with a big smile, "Nope, you're all wrong. Life is dangerous!" Then, in case we didn't hear him the first time, he repeated, "Life is dangerous!" He told us, "You are all afraid — scared of the people sitting next to you, in front of you, at work, at school, the people on the streets, the people you don't know — everywhere in the world, all of them. You're frightened of them and they're frightened of you too."

For some reason, the word 'dangerous' wasn't too broad of a concept, but 'awesome' was clearly over the top.

At this point I was thinking, *This is complete nonsense!* I turned to the girl next to me, who was in her mid-20s, and said, "I want you to know that I'm not scared of you, and I hope you aren't frightened of me, because I'm not a scary guy and this world is an amazing, beautiful place and is rarely dangerous." She smiled and assured me that she was definitely not afraid of me.

That session illustrates one of the most important lessons I've learned about happiness:

It Is Exactly What You Think It Is

TRUTH!

Whatever dominates your thoughts: that is how you live your life. In other words, you get whatever you focus on with intensity for prolonged periods of time. This works all the time, every time, good and bad, for everyone.

You say that life is dangerous? You'll see danger everywhere.

You say that life is heartbreak? Even in your best relationships, you'll be looking ahead to the moment that it will all come to a tragic, bitter end rather than expecting and enjoying the best that it already is.

Have you ever known people who are 'victims'? They expect bad things to happen, and they do. Bad luck seems to follow them around. If you listen to these people, they ask themselves questions like, "Why do bad things always happen to me? What terrible thing is going to happen next? Why can't I catch a break?"

You get what you focus on, and you also get the answers to the questions that you ask.

What do you think would happen if 'victims' asked themselves questions that they might actually want the answers to — like, "How can I make this happen?

What if things worked out perfectly, what would that look and feel like?"

If you are consumed by the thought of terrible things happening, they will continue to happen. If you want to change what happens to you, it starts by changing how you think.

And if you want to be happy, you have to learn how to think differently. You need to think like happy people think.

Life At The Basic Level

Think of babies: when they're born they experience very few emotions. But they *react* to emotions they see on the adult faces around them — that's how they learn the different emotional states that extend beyond pain and pleasure (satiation).

Researchers believe that within the first three months babies can express and react to five basic emotions: joy, interest, anger, sadness, and disgust.[5]

As they continue to grow, babies' emotions develop and they start to link particular emotions to particular people, actions, and physical feelings. *I believe that these links are the beginnings of the vital interconnection between our thoughts and our emotions.*

Are there emotions that we can feel without any thoughts? Yes — and no. The human response to danger is known as the 'fight, flight, or freeze' reaction.

This reaction has been shown to occur before the cognitive mind kicks in and produces even the fastest thought. So we can feel the rush of adrenaline that we call fear before we actually recognize danger cognitively.

But for the most part, our emotions are triggered by our thoughts. We see someone we love and have the thought, "It's _____!" And the emotion of love/happiness/pleasure occurs. We see someone or

something that we dislike, have the thought, "It's
____," and the emotion of dislike/disgust pops up.

We also can simply think about someone we love
or dislike, or a situation that scares us, and we will
feel that corresponding emotion — without actually
being near that person or in that situation! Our feelings are greatly influenced by our thoughts that stimulate chemical releases in our brain. This happens all
the time naturally, whether we're aware of it or not,
24-hours a day, even while we sleep. Our thoughts
are inexorably and intrinsically linked to our emotions.
And the great news is that this means **we can use
our thoughts to direct and shape the emotions we
experience.**

(For a greater insight into the scientific function
of thoughts and how they relate to happiness and
pleasure, I recommend reading *The Science of Happiness* by Stefan Klein. See the *Positive Psychology
Research* section in the back of this book for more
information.)

The problem though, is with our ultra-powerful
survival instinct that makes negative thoughts and
emotions more 'important' than the positive ones.
We are always unconsciously looking for danger and
how to avoid it. That's why negative emotions dom-
inate our psyche and are much stronger and easily
accessible than positive emotions — it's the 'save the
organism' auto-response that we all have.

So knowing this, how can we think ourselves happy? How do we train our minds and bodies to be

content, and to make happiness our default setting? This is not just about finding happy moments or creating happy moments and locking them in. It's how to make 'happy & fulfilled' your automatic default setting, instead of 'worry & scarcity'.

We can think ourselves happy by **actively taking control of our thoughts and emotions.** Thoughts control our feelings, which influence our actions. Without control of our thoughts, we are stimulated by outside circumstances, and we react rather than respond.

When we choose to direct our thoughts, we can calm the chemical storms racing through our bodies. We can move ourselves from fear to awareness, anger to focus, disappointment to reflection, and satisfaction to active happiness and joy — simply by changing our thoughts, or choosing what to think in any situation.

"Easier said than done," I can hear you saying. True, but there is a way to condition ourselves to think in such a way that we are happier more often. Like any other learned behavior, thinking yourself happy takes training, practice, and some discipline. But believe me, the rewards are worth it. With a little practice,when someone asks you, "What's life like?" you too will want to yell out loud,

"IT'S F*CKING AWESOME!"

Chapter Summary

✦ Whatever dominates your thoughts is how you live your life. You get whatever you intensely focus on for prolonged periods of time.

✦ If you want to be happy, you have to learn how to think differently. You can condition yourself to be happier by following specific proven methods.

✦ You can think yourself happy by actively taking control of your thoughts and emotions.

WHAT TO DO NEXT:

<u>**WATCH THIS VIDEO**</u>

✦www.ThinkYourselfHappy.com/Chapter-2

3

The Five Changes To Think Yourself Happy

"Most folks are as happy
as they make their minds up to be."
— **Abraham Lincoln**

Happiness, along with all your emotions, is a product of your thoughts. The way you think about yourself, your life, your relationships, your work, and the world in general affects your emotions dramatically.

However, it's not quite as simple as just waking up in the morning and thinking, "Okay, I'm happy!" To think yourself happy requires a system. It means you have to make *five specific changes* in the way you think so happiness becomes your default response to the world.

But even before you learn the specifics of this system, you need to identify what's important to you and what drives you. To get where you want to go, you not only have to know where you're going, but you also need to know where you are right now. *Clarity* is where it all starts.

Once you know what you want, you can figure how to get there — and the thoughts and emotions you'd like to have along the way. The answers we get in life come from the questions we ask ourselves and others. Here are some questions you must eventually answer. I suggest you look them over now and spend a little time thinking about them. The answers will clarify what ultimately drives you. Whatever drives you will have a big impact on your thoughts, your actions, and ultimately, your happiness.

QUESTION 1:

Who Am I, And What Do I Want?

What's important to me? What would I do with my time if money weren't a factor? Am I spending time in the areas of my life that I enjoy the most and bring the most fulfillment? What would my best life look like?

These questions help you determine the conditions that would make it easy for you to be happy. They'll also give you an idea of your current happiness level and start you thinking about ways you can increase it.

QUESTION 2:

Who Do I Want To Become?

If I were on my deathbed and looking back on my life, who would I want to have been during the course of my lifetime? Was I kind, successful, loved and loving, creative, admired, and supportive? Was I a leader, and driven? Looking at my life now, is there a gap between who I want to become and who I am currently?

To become someone new, or an expanded version of who you are now, you need to be a person you've never been. Once you are that person, you'll be living that life. This doesn't mean pretending to be different than you are. This means upgrading you to 'the best you that you can be' according to your standards, not the standards of others. Purposefully shaping your character will allow even more amazing opportunities to enter your life.

QUESTION 3:

What Would Life Be Like If I Were Happier?

Would I be nicer to the people around me? More focused and creative? A better boss, leader, employee, contractor? Would my family enjoy my company more and all be closer? Could I be healthier and my stress level lower? Would I get out of bed in the morning with excitement and pleasure, and go to bed at night feeling more fulfilled and at peace?

All of that is possible if you're willing to put in the work to change the way you think. It's not complicated rocket science, nor do you have to meditate for hours (although I recommend daily meditation for a lot of reasons). You don't have to become a vegan. You won't lose your drive or edge or whatever you call the force you believe has made you successful in the past. In fact, I've found that thinking yourself happy can actually make you more driven and successful simply because you feel better about yourself and the people on your team will enjoy being around you more... guaranteed!

But you do have to break some long-standing bad thinking habits and adopt a few new ones. Luckily, these new habits aren't like quitting smoking or going on a diet — there's little to no pain or deprivation involved. But you do need to be able to catch yourself when you're falling into old negative thought patterns and change your approach in that moment. Don't beat yourself up, just stop once you recognize it, and move forward with the right actions.

Here are five changes you can make to your thinking that will create greater happiness immediately. In fact, making any of these five changes will increase your level of happiness, and doing all five will explode your happiness beyond anything you might believe possible.

Retraining your brain does take consistent application of these new ways of thinking. With a small amount of sustained effort over the course of a month, you can retrain your brain to be happier and make your life much better as a result.

Let's take a look at the five changes to think yourself happy. It starts with **Visualization.**

Chapter Summary

✧ To think yourself happy requires a system. Every one of these strategies is proven to work. The more you do, the happier you'll become.

✧ You must get clear on what's important to you. Answer these questions:

　　1) Who am I, and what do I want?

　　2) Who do I want to become?

　　3) What would my life be like if I were happy every day?

✧ When you realize you are falling into old habits, stop doing it, then move on. It's a process.

WHAT TO DO NEXT:

<u>WATCH THIS VIDEO</u>

✧ www.ThinkYourselfHappy.com/Chapter-3

4
Change #1: Visualization

*"Create a vision of who you want to be,
then live into that picture as if it were
already true."*
— **Arnold Schwarzenegger**

In 2007, two researchers at Bishop's University tested the effects of visualization on the body. They studied college athletes by putting them in to three groups. The first group went to the gym and worked out to train their hip flexor muscles. The second group did no exercise, only visualizing working their hip flexors. The control group did neither physical exercise nor visualization.

The study lasted for two weeks. At the end of that time, while the control group hadn't improved at all, the athletes that went to the gym had increased their hip strength by 28 percent. The athletes that only *visualized* working out had increased their hip strength by 24 percent — almost as much, without lifting a weight or using a machine![6]

That's the power of visualization. The brain can't tell the difference between an event you've imagined clearly, with emotion, and something that actually happened. When you see it as though it's already done, your nervous system is getting used to you accomplishing that task. It will make it easier to replicate again and again, so when you take the physical action, it will already feel natural and doable.

Not long ago, my wife Rocky and I were having an adventure week in Queenstown, New Zealand, which happens to be the extreme adventure capital of the world. Rocky has, in the past, committed to doing things considered daring and dangerous, but then, due to fear, was unable to pull it together and bailed out at the last second.

She decided this time that she was going to take on the tallest bungee jump in New Zealand, the Nevis Gorge, at 440 feet, so being the awesome supportive husband I am, I said, "Sure baby, let's go!" By the time we arrived at the welcome center, she was a wreck and trying very hard not to cry.

She looked at me and said, "I'm scared, but I have to do this."

I said, "No, you don't. You know you don't."

She said, "Yeah, but I'm going to. I'm really going to do this."

I said, "There is no reason to jump. You have to have a purpose or you're going to be scared. Falling off the ledge or jumping off doesn't matter. Those are just style points for your ego. The execution is all that matters.

I have a secret that most people on the planet don't know about bungy jumping. The energy it creates makes it possible to fly — I mean, really fly. The real magic happens after the jump. When the downward momentum comes to a stop, the negative energy reverses and there's a massive burst of positive energy that is created. There's an opportunity in that precise moment to use that positive energy to your advantage and not just let it just dissipate and be wasted."

I said, "Focus on coiling into a tight ball so when the time comes, you can uncoil with your own burst of energy, adding to this new power that's been created, and you'll be able to fly unrestricted through the air like Superwoman... totally safe."

As I finished, I saw Rocky wasn't shaking anymore. Her mind had shifted to accomplishing a result she was now excited about. She said, "I love it! I've got this!"

I drew an imaginary line with my foot and stood next to her. Then, I grabbed the back of her jacket with a firm grip and said, "I want you to put your toes on that line that I just drew and focus on what you need to do to achieve your outcome. And don't look down. This needs to feel real."

Together we practiced what it was going to be like. Over and over we jumped, visualizing the perfect execution. Then I stepped back and just watched.

The bus arrived and we began the hours-long ride to the jump site. Rocky wasn't saying a word. When we arrived, Rocky walked off by herself to a quiet, flat spot and drew a line in the dirt with her foot. I watched her take a deep breath, step up to that line with laser focus, and jump with determination, over and over.

Rocky asked to be first, and after a quick, confident smile, she stepped up to the ledge for the countdown. Three, two, one — and she dove off that platform with purpose, free and unrestricted she flew... and there was no fear, only excitement.

As humans, we have the unique ability to play out any scenario in our brain that we choose. We can visualize something happening and our nervous system processes it the same way, whether it's made up or actually happening — we have the same visceral reactions. This can work to our advantage or disadvantage. We can feel great and excited when we see ourselves succeeding. We also can feel afraid and discouraged if all we can picture is failure.

I'd grown up having rich friends, but no access to money, and I'd think about how fun and easy life would be once I became a multi-millionaire. I'd cut out photos from magazines of super high-end cars, jets, yachts, and mansions on the beach and tape them to my walls and mirrors so I could actually see myself with these things and would get accustomed to having them around.

That may sound silly to you — but not if you've ever done it yourself. To this day, this is a practice I recommend because it yields such stunning results. Visualization of success is a process utilized by most high achievers. I've never met anyone who's done this and not had at least some of these items show up in their lives. I sure have.

To attract the things in your life that you want, you must visualize them first. The clearer the picture, the stronger the pull there is to making that happen. Focus on these pictures intensely and often. See them in your mind's eye, as if they're on their way, and then see them as though they're already part of your everyday life. The same feelings will follow whether you are visualizing success or actually creating it. However, the same process also works for bad events that happened in the past or that you're worried may happen. You see it and feel it, and often you manage to create it in your life. Or you feel the drag of past bad events that puts a damper on your emotions and drive. That isn't where you want to live. So practice visualizing yourself the way you want to be. See your success. Above all, see yourself happily moving through the process, not happy later.

Athletes use visualization all the time. Michael Phelps, the incredible US swimmer who's won 28 Olympic medals (23 gold), visualizes every moment of every single race he swims before he even swims it. His coach, Bob Bowman, calls it "putting in the videotape." Every night and every morning, Phelps rehearses his upcoming race. He sees himself walking out to the pool, standing on the block, getting into position, jumping in the water. He sees and feels every stroke, every breath — right up until the moment he touches the wall ahead of everyone else.

Phelps also visualizes what to do when things go wrong, like the time at the Beijing Olympics in 2008 when his goggles leaked and he had to swim an entire race completely blind. (He still won the gold, by the way.) But what he never visualizes is failing to achieve his goal. He uses his mind to create the physical, mental, and emotional habits of success.[7]

The process of visualizing exactly what you want — and the feeling of already having it — is something we all should practice and master.

EXERCISE:
Visualize The Best And Worst-Case Scenarios

Think about something you want to create in the future. It can be a new job or promotion, a new client, a better relationship, a fit and trim body — something that would be important to you.

Now, see yourself already having achieved that particular goal. Visualize yourself in the new job, or signing the new client. See and feel what your life is like with an even more deep and meaningful relationship. See and feel yourself with that strong, fit, powerful, trim body, and feel what that body is like as you move confidently. Create powerful, positive feelings of happiness at being the person who has this particular goal in your life.

This is your best-case scenario. Feels great, doesn't it? But remember, your thoughts can make you feel lousy if you don't direct them in a positive way that works for you, not against you.

Try this experiment: See yourself having tried to reach your goal, but failing. Visualize the worst-case scenario— someone else gets the job, the client tells you there's no way they'll hire you, your significant other turns a cold shoulder to all your efforts to improve your relationship, and try as you might, you can't seem to lose the weight or get fit.

How do you feel? Defeated? Depressed? Worried? Angry? Frustrated? Sad? That's the power of your mind making you feel terrible — *even though nothing bad has actually happened!*

In later chapters, you'll learn how to turn your thinking around even when things aren't going your way, but for now, let's change this up and use your thoughts to visualize a different future. See yourself having overcome all the obstacles you faced in the worst-case scenario. Someone else got the job? You go out and find a better one. The client says no? Tell them thanks for considering you, and then close two new clients. Your significant other rebuffs your efforts to be closer? See yourself doing something so incredible that they're astounded by your passion and commitment and they fall into your arms.

You don't make your weight goal? Visualize trying something else that's exactly what you need to drop the pounds or gain the level of fitness you want — a new hobby, activity, way of eating, or lifestyle choice. Then see yourself walking triumphantly down the street, having overcome obstacles that you thought were impossible, and happy beyond measure at your success.

Shakespeare once wrote, "There's nothing either good or bad, but thinking makes it so." Visualizing is your ticket to making yourself happy, by creating pictures of what you want and then letting yourself feel the happiness of becoming someone who's living that way. In the next chapter we'll talk about the second change: **Positive Anticipation.**

Chapter Summary

- Your brain can't tell the difference between an event you've imagined clearly (with emotion) and something that actually happened.

- To understand the power of visualization, picture the best-case and worst-case scenarios for something you wish to happen. Notice the power of your mind to make you feel great or terrible.

- To attract the things you want in your life, you must visualize them first. The clearer the picture, the stronger the pull.

WHAT TO DO NEXT:

WATCH THIS VIDEO

www.ThinkYourselfHappy.com/Chapter-4

5

Change #2: Positive Anticipation

"An intense anticipation itself transforms possibility into reality."
— **Samuel Smiles**

Remember a time when you really looked forward to something. The night before your wedding... The day before a big race... The time you started college or went to a new school or a new job... Or maybe you were awaiting the birth of your first child. Do you remember the butterflies, the excitement, and the happiness? Even though the event hadn't happened yet, you were in a state of *positive anticipation* because you knew something great was on its way. You can attach these same feelings to any situation that may be in your future and use them to make yourself happy — and to make your success more likely.

How does this work? Positive anticipation builds confidence and certainty. Once you've visualized success in your mind and celebrated your victory in advance, you know you can do it. This is different from thinking you might be able to do something, because you have proof inside yourself. In your mind's eye, you've seen yourself win and already felt what it was like — so, of course, you can achieve the same success again.

Along with positive anticipation is the idea of delayed gratification. The ability to embrace delayed gratification, or the development of that skill, has been scientifically proven to be a strong indicator of happiness throughout those people's lives. There was a professor at Stanford University named Walter Mischel who conducted a famous study that lasted 40 years and was known as 'The Marshmallow Experiment'. The study was done on hundreds of children ages 4–5 years old. Mischel and his team brought each child into a private room one at a time and sat them at a table. A single marshmallow was placed in front of them and the children were told they could eat the marshmallow or wait until the researcher got back and then get a second marshmallow for waiting or, if they ate it before the researcher returned, got nothing more. Then the researcher left the room for 15 minutes.

Over the next 40 years, this same experiment was studied and tracked and here's what it showed. The children who delayed gratification were markedly more successful in a wide variety of areas. The ones who waited and got the second marshmallow were better able to use positive anticipation, and that carried through their lives. This group had lower rates of substance abuse and lower rates of obesity, they responded better to stress, and scored higher on college entrance exams. The published abstract on the study states, "To function effectively, individuals must voluntarily postpone immediate gratification and persist in goal-directed behavior for the sake of later outcomes."[8]

Remember Michael Phelps' visualizations of each race he swims? Phelps doesn't stop his visualization with the sight, sounds, and feelings of touching the wall. He also sees his head coming out of the water, ripping off his swim cap, looking up at the timer on the wall, seeing a recordsetting time, and then celebrating his victory. He creates positive anticipation for his success every time he mentally rehearses a race. This practice reduces the negative effects of 'lagtime' which is the time between taking the right action, and receiving the desired result. No longer will waiting be the hardest part.

Remember, when you see it as though it's already happened, your nervous system is getting used to you accomplishing that task and will make it easier for you to replicate success again and again. Then, when you actually take the physical action, it will already feel natural and doable.

So before you ever get started, make a practice of visualizing yourself as being successful at whatever you attempt. Like Michael Phelps, every night and morning, 'run the videotape' of whatever you need to accomplish. See every moment and feel it fully. Then you too will find yourself standing on top of the podium with your version of a gold medal – whatever that victory is for you.

Exercise:
Positive Anticipation

Imagine that it's next New Year's Eve and you're at a party with your closest friends and family — all the people you love and care about, and who love and care for you. Someone proposes that each person in the group stands up and describes his or her past year.

You listen to your friends and family talk about the successes and challenges they've experienced and you reflect on their stories.

Now it's your turn. You stand up and start to describe the past year. What do you say?

Of course, it's not New Year's Eve and you're describing events that haven't happened yet — or, if they have, your perspective on those events is completely in your control. (More on **Perspective** in Change #4.)

Therefore, you can choose to make your year a victory celebration, celebrating all that you've become and all that you've made happen for yourself and others. On the other hand, you can imagine the worst disaster possible — your personal nightmare of a year, whatever that is.

Good or bad, neither has happened. So, after feeling both in your mind and your body, which feeling serves you and which doesn't? Since most of those events haven't happened yet, you get to choose what it will be like when they do. Choose to feel good about what's coming — it's more fun, and a lot less stressful!

Now you'll learn about the effects of **meaning** upon your thinking — and your emotions.

Chapter Summary

✤ Positive anticipation builds confidence and certainty. Once you've visualized success in your mind and celebrated your victory in advance, you know you can do it.

✤ Along with positive anticipation, the all-important practice of delayed gratification is crucial. This makes lagtime enjoyable because you feel good things coming.

✤ When you visualize your success with positive anticipation, your nervous system is getting used to you succeeding and will make it easier for you to do it again and again.

WHAT TO DO NEXT:

WATCH THIS VIDEO

✤www.ThinkYourselfHappy.com/Chapter-5

6
Change #3: Meaning

"Nothing in life has any meaning except the meaning you give it."
— **Tony Robbins**

Imagine you are a 35-year-old executive and one day you walk into your office holding onto the old, ratty teddy bear you used to take to bed every night as a child. People would think you were crazy — and they'd be right. Yet how many of us are still holding on to some really old, ratty stories from our past that continue to make us miserable?

As humans, we live out the stories we make up for ourselves. And the meaning we assign to whatever happens in our lives affects everything we do and don't do. The problem is that most of us choose to tell ourselves some really lousy stories — again, and again, and again. For example, you had a relationship that imploded. Or a business venture that failed. Or a college you didn't get into. Or you blew a race or a game. Or you lost someone that you cared about deeply. All too often, people hang onto the pain of these pieces of the past for years and let these incidents shape their lives for the worse.

Things that happened in the past have hurt you enough. Don't let them continue to do damage by continuing to give them energy in your thoughts. Although these emotionally significant events did occur, they aren't happening now — and you can choose not to keep reliving them. This is the story of you — who you are and why you are the way you are. What's the story and meaning you've given to the events that have happened in your past?

Although you can't change the events of your past, you can always choose to change what those events mean, and how they affect you. Re-examine the beliefs you have around those stories that may be holding you back. If your story is that someone you loved left — and therefore you're sure that everyone you love in the future will leave, too — how would that belief cause you to treat the people trying to get close to you?

Change the meaning. Someone you loved left. That means they had to go, and that's all. This is where you can choose to believe that everything happens for a reason and it's for your benefit.

The Universe conspires for you, not against you. I believe that. If you believe that, how would you approach your day? How could that affect the way you view obstacles and so-called problems? If it's really true that life is ultimately on your side, what should you attempt? And how much happier could you be regardless of circumstances?

The mind can only occupy one space in time, so choose to fill your mind with active thoughts that move you in the direction you want to go, not to the place you want to stay away from. If something is coming up and you can't bear the thought of what might be, then don't. The event hasn't even happened yet, so don't live the worst thoughts as though they're real now.

If we let it, our minds will take us through the worst possible scenarios — ones that could never be possible — and emotionally, we get to live through every one of those visions as though they actually happened. That's ugly, and you don't have to do that.

Choose to believe things will work out for the best every time, and whatever comes to fruition, will only happen once. But until then, choose a story that works for you, not against you. Choose a powerful meaning and you'll take back the power over your own life.

Exercise:
Change The Meaning Of A Past Event

Think of a past event that was really a bummer. It could be something relatively small, like getting picked last for a sports team when you were a little kid, or something big, like the time you got fired, or dumped by your soul mate, or a trauma you experienced as a child or adult, or the death or injury of someone you loved.

What meaning did you give that event at the time? Was it one that made you feel better, or worse?

Often we give events the worst possible meaning immediately after they happen, when we're in the middle of very powerful negative emotions like anger, sadness, fear, hurt, guilt, or shame.

Your emotions influence the meanings you assign to those events. But that was then and this is now — and today you can choose to change the meaning of any event by changing how you think about it.

Looking back at that past event, is there another meaning you can give it based on what you've learned and experienced since then? Maybe getting picked last for the sports team made you work harder and become a better athlete. Or perhaps it caused you to pursue other activities — like computers, or literature, or music — that you excel at and enjoy a whole lot more.

Maybe getting fired put you on the path of a different career, or caused you to move to a different city, or helped you decide to become an entrepreneur and never have to work for someone again. Maybe your soul mate leaving made you get really clear about what you needed to do and who you needed to be in order to be a great partner, and have a great partner.

If you *had* to put a positive meaning on that event, what could it be? Perhaps your past event was the loss of a loved one, and the pain of their passing is still strong. If your loved one were standing in front of you right now, what do you believe he or she would tell you that you should believe about their passing? Would they want you to hold onto the pain you feel, or would they ask you to remember them with love and use that memory to honor them and make your life great?

If you still find yourself hanging on to the pain of that past event, try looking at the event from the perspective of God or the Universe, or whatever you believe generates reality. From the Universe's perspective — and knowing that the Universe conspires for us, not against us — what could be a positive and powerful meaning of this past event?

Now, some events are incredibly difficult to find a positive meaning for, I understand. There are things no human being should have to go through. But if you keep reliving the event and continue to experience the pain of it again and again, you're never going to be free of it and your happiness will continue to be affected negatively.

You deserve better. If necessary, get some professional help from an excellent therapist, there are some. Find someone who can walk you through letting go of the feelings holding you back and help you discover new meanings that will allow you to move forward.

Our thoughts and feelings should be under our control. But thoughts, like breathing, can be controlled consciously or unconsciously.

You can actually stimulate yourself to feel anything you decide to by assigning a meaning of your own choosing to any past, present, or future event.

When you really get this, when you understand that you can choose the meaning of any event. You'll feel more in control of your life, and the happier you'll be.

To develop a better meaning often requires us to look at the past, present, or future from a different **Perspective.** That's the next step to thinking yourself

Chapter Summary

- As humans, we live out the stories we make up for ourselves. However, most of us tell ourselves some really lousy stories.

- Although you can't change the events of your past, you can always choose to change what those events mean. If you had to put a positive meaning on a past event, what would it be?

- Choose positive meanings for the events that happen to you and you'll gain control of your life and your happiness.

WHAT TO DO NEXT:

<u>**WATCH THIS VIDEO**</u>

- www.ThinkYourselfHappy.com/Chapter-6

7
Change #4: Perspective

"There are no facts, only interpretations."
— **Friedrich Nietzsche**

My son, Tanner, has a friend whose dad is a well-known celebrity. When the boys were both in high school, Tanner's friend was at our house complaining that someone had stepped on his new shoes earlier that day. He was still very upset about the incident, even several hours later. Tanner commented that he had only two pair of casual shoes and told his friend not to complain about a small dirt spot on one of his more than 50 perfect pairs of shoes. Then Dillon, Tanner's twin brother, said he had only one pair of shoes with several holes in them and that he loved them and didn't want new ones.

As I listened, I remembered visiting villages in Fiji where no one owns any shoes and yet everyone has huge smiles on their faces nearly all the time. Come to think of it, I remember people there with no legs, happy as can be. And here's this kid who has everything he could want but chooses to focus his thoughts on a time when his shoe got dirty. I suggested he clean off his shoe and move on with gratitude for the abundance in his life. (I don't think he got it.)

You can use perspective to change how you feel by internalizing various possibilities of how your situation could be much worse than it is. You can also help ease a painful situation by exploring the possibilities of how you could be happy even in those circumstances.

Some people use the phrase "Well, at least..." as a way to change their perspective on something that made them unhappy. You had a fight with your spouse? Well, at least you stopped it before it escalated out of control. You're being audited by the IRS? Hey, at least you made enough money last year that they thought you were worth auditing. If you can inject some humor into the situation, even better. One of the best tools I've found to develop a new perspective is to ask a question that makes you focus on whatever makes you happy. Here are a few examples.

- How amazing is my life right now compared to where it could be?

- Several years ago, would I have considered this a great problem to have?

- Is this a problem or an opportunity?

- Ten years from now, will I really care about this?

- In the grand scheme of things, how much does this really matter?

- What can I learn from this?

One question I learned to ask a long time ago is, "What's great about this?" Simply asking can cause you to look at the situation in a different way. If your manager embezzled funds from the business and vanished, aren't you glad he or she's gone and can no longer steal from you?

Maybe what's great is that now you'll have to dig in and go through your books thoroughly for the first time in years — and you might find new ways to make or save money that you never would've discovered.

Questions will change your life when you come up with the right answers. The answers are always there; you just need to ask effectively — in ways that serve and empower you. Stay away from negative questions such as "Why can't I?" or "Why don't things ever work out?" It's better to ask "How can I?"

And remember to frame your questions and statements so they're positive and beneficial to your desired outcome.

For example, if you tell a child, "Don't spill your drink," what usually ends up happening? The kid ends up spilling the drink. A better choice of words would be "Make sure to keep your drink in your cup, please." This reinforces the action you desire rather than focusing on what you don't want to happen.

There are always things to be grateful for, and situations could always be worse. Make the decision to spend less time being unhappy by changing your perspective.

Events happen that aren't pleasant and they're going to knock us down, but don't stay there — get up and do something.

If you think about and do things you enjoy, you'll be happy. If you spend time thinking about the things that make you sad, you'll feel sad. I suggest that whenever you find yourself unhappy, take the perspective that unhappiness means your situation needs to change.

Exercise:
Gain A New Perspective

Whenever you find yourself in a less-than-optimal circumstance, take a moment to look at things from a different perspective.

Ask yourself, "What's great about this?" or "What *could* be great about this?"

Try a question like "Will this even matter in ten minutes, ten hours, ten days, or ten years?" (I use that question a lot when it comes to other drivers on the freeway.)

See if you can find humor in the situation: "Wow, I never knew someone could be that bad a driver!" Or use the phrase "Well, it could be worse—I could be..." and then come up with something absurd, like "I could be stuck in quicksand without any vines hanging around to pull myself out!" Or my favorite: "At least I'm not ____." (Insert someone you are happy not to be.)

A totally different perspective allows growth and contribution. It's a way of looking at yourself as a problem solver, doing your part to be solution oriented rather than problem oriented. So many people are stuck in their own story, or so focused on their personal situation, that they don't see the bigger picture. They aren't aware that the problems they've encountered and overcome are the stories of inspiration and motivation that others need to help pull them through their painful situations. There's no better feeling than helping out someone who wants to become more. When you're part of something bigger than yourself that leaves a legacy of helping others, then you've found one of life's greatest gifts.

Anything that puts your situation in a different perspective can help you be happier, or, if not happier, at least on a more even keel with your situation.

Remember that happiness is a choice, so change your perspective and take action immediately to do what you can to create the circumstances you want.

One of the easiest ways to change your perspective is to thank your lucky stars every day for the gifts in your life. That's what the last step is all about: **Gratitude.**

Chapter Summary

⬦ You can use perspective to change how you feel by internalizing various other possibilities.

⬦ Asking a question that makes you focus on whatever makes you happy is a great tool to develop a new perspective. Questions will change your life when you ask questions that serve and empower you. "How can I be part of something greater than myself?"

⬦ Whenever you find yourself in difficult circumstances, ask yourself, "What's great about this?", "What *could* be great about this?", and "What have I learned that will help me later?"

WHAT TO DO NEXT:

<u>**WATCH THIS VIDEO**</u>

⬦ www.ThinkYourselfHappy.com/Chapter-7

8
Change #5: Gratitude

"The more you recognize and express gratitude for the things you have, the more things you will have to express gratitude for."
— **Zig Ziglar**

Gratitude is appreciation in the now. It's love for what is. Living in gratitude is the perpetual act of being thankful. This state is also one of the deepest, most meaningful, and sustainable forms of happiness there is. And this feeling is available to you at any time you choose.

Science is finally starting to research the powerful effects that gratitude can have on our health and happiness.

For Example:

- Grateful people are healthier and report fewer aches and pains.

- Experiencing gratitude decreases toxic emotions like frustration, regret, envy, and anger. It also raises self-esteem and reduces our tendency to compare ourselves to others.

- Gratitude fosters resilience and helps people deal with trauma and setbacks.[9]

- Finally, according to Robert Emmons, PhD, a professor of psychology and a positive psychology scholar, regular grateful thinking can increase our happiness by at least 25%.[10]

In the words of Epicurus, *"Do not spoil what you have by desiring what you have not; remember that what you now have was once among the things you only hoped for."*

Take a moment and think of three things you're grateful for in your life — perhaps three things that were once only a dream, but now you've turned into reality. Hold a clear picture of them in your mind and notice how you feel about them. Feel thankful for these things right now. Think of nothing other than how happy you are that these things, people, and situations exist in your life — just for you, right now.

I use the power of gratitude every day. Whenever I'm feeling frustrated or overwhelmed, it moves me from negative feelings to being humble and appreciating everything I have, am, and experience. Gratitude also helps me in my closest relationships. Somehow it's very easy to get upset with family members simply because they're closest to us and we're in proximity to them more often — and for whatever reason, they seem to be really good at pushing our buttons! But gratitude can help us get past the upset and recognize how much we love these people, even if they're upsetting us in the moment.

Whenever I have a challenge with things, people, situations, or opportunities, I think about what I'm grateful for and I remember that my family and friends are always at the top of my gratitude list. I don't let the opportunity go by to tell a loved one that I love and appreciate them. When I think of it, I act on it and make a phone call or send a text to let them know. If you don't tell them, they won't know.

You can use gratitude to pull yourself out of a mental rut, or bad mood. It can lift you up from anger and help you through grief.

Gratitude will eliminate thoughts of "Why me?" or "Why not me?" It will center you right where you need to be when you need to be there. It's free, easy, and beneficial.

Researchers at several major universities have proven the undeniable power of gratitude: In one study done at University of Pennsylvania, Dr. Martin Seligman tested the impact of gratitude with 411 subjects. Two groups, one a control group, were given an assignment to write about an early memory. The non-control group was asked to write and personally deliver a thank you letter to someone who'd never properly been thanked for their kindness. Participants immediately exhibited a huge jump in their happiness score, with benefits lasting up to a month. The control group who did nothing, received no benefit.

Researchers at the Wharton School at the University of Pennsylvania divided telephone fundraisers into two groups. One was thanked by the managers for their work, and the other group wasn't. The group shown gratitude made 50% more fundraising calls.

Most of us recognize the power of gratitude and we intend to feel it more often, but because we're overstimulated all day and busy doing other things, we can forget to be grateful.

So how can we remind ourselves to be grateful more often? In order to effectively create a habit, you must repeat the same activity regularly for at least a month (no big deal). So do the following three practices for the next 30-days.

Exercise:
Three Gratitude Practices

#1: Starting today, think of two things you're grateful for. Every day, add at least two more items to that list. After 30-days, you'll have a glorious list.

#2: When you wake up from any sleep, **before you get up,** do two things. First, be grateful. Be grateful for waking up, this means you are alive, a great way to start every day! Then think of your list of things you're grateful for and be happy about each one that you remember. Add any new things you find yourself grateful for.

#3: From there, prepare to get moving with intention. **Before you stand up,** have a vision in mind for how you'd like your day to go. Be specific. What are you putting out into the world? Who's counting on you, and how are you showing up for them? Feel grateful to have the opportunity to create the day you've envisioned that lies ahead for you. Be clear about your intentions, and make things happen in a big way, with enthusiasm, confidence, and energy!

Take on this gratitude practice and your life will change massively. In 30-days you'll have it, and you'll want to continue this practice for the rest of your life.

You get to choose how to feel, so why wouldn't you start every day being grateful and directed?

Chapter Summary

✤ Gratitude is appreciation in the now. It's also one of the deepest, most meaningful, and sustainable forms of happiness there is.

✤ Remind yourself to be grateful more often.

✤ Start your day with a gratitude practice. Before you get out of bed, think of things you're grateful for and be happy about each of them. Then have a vision in mind for how you'd like your day to go?

WHAT TO DO NEXT:

<u>**WATCH THIS VIDEO**</u>

✤www.ThinkYourselfHappy.com/Chapter-8

9

Conclusion: The Science of Happily Achieving

*"The Constitution only gives people
the right to pursue happiness.
You have to catch it yourself."*
— **Benjamin Franklin**

You now have the five changes in thinking that will immediately improve your life. You must change your thinking through visualization, positive anticipation, choosing your meanings, perspective, and gratitude. When you practice any of these five changes regularly (try doing them for 30-straight days so they become a habit) you too can **think yourself happy.**

Not only will you be making yourself happier, but you also will be conditioning your brain to create greater results for yourself. You see, a long time ago I came up with what I believe is the universal formula for success. It starts with right thinking — and with these five changes, you'll be on the path to getting your thinking headed in the right direction.

Right Thinking
1. Visualization
2. Positive Anticipation
3. Meaning
4. Perspective
5. Gratitude

Follow Through
1. Prepare
2. Plan
3. Execute
4. Measure
5. Improve

Follow these practices, and over time, you'll master the success mindset. But right thinking is nothing without follow through, without practice, without active effort.

That's why the **Universal Success Formula™** looks like this:

Right Thinking + Follow Through = Success

These paradigms of thinking are developed and strengthened over time; if you follow through and practice them regularly, you're conditioning yourself to feel fantastic every day, both in your mind and body. Then you'll more consistently take the right actions in life that'll lead to the success you want.

At first, it isn't easy to remember to do the things that benefit us, but ultimately, once you start implementing these short, proven happiness strategies, you'll immediately notice a massive improvement in every area of your life. These results will happen without any lag time. Not only will you feel like you can have anything you want at any time, but you'll actually feel like you already have those things, be grateful that you do, and celebrate — because your brain and body won't know the difference.

If you follow the ideas in this book, you'll discover how easy it can be to make happiness a regular part of your daily life. And when you do, you'll also discover how much faster you can achieve the results you want to produce when you're happy — while you're working on them.

You're going to have amazing success with these five changes in thinking, no doubt.

However, there's one more thing I want to talk to you about that you need to be aware of... the things you say. As your thoughts can flow freely without notice, so can your words. And I'm not just talking about the things you say out loud. The most damaging words are usually what you say to yourself.

Don't be so hard on yourself and others. Be kind — give yourself and others a break. People are doing the best they can with the skills and tools they have. Talk to yourself as if you were writing notes to your first grade self.

Be encouraging, supportive, and positive. You wouldn't write a note to a kid that they're ugly — or fat or stupid or a loser or not good enough. Many people bully themselves more than they realize. It's time to end that now.

Don't let that be you. You deserve to be happy, so give yourself the break you deserve and become your own best friend. Look in the mirror and verbalize what's awesome, unique, and amazing about you. You're a winner! Figure out your gifts and shine onto the world.

There's no one like you — rock it!

Think about anything you want to accomplish or create:

How much more fun would it be if you made it a point to be happy before you started and while you're working on it?

Why in the world should you have to wait to be happy and celebrate?

Won't the effort be a lot more fun if you're celebrating and are happy every step of the way?

My hope is that you enjoy this process and share it with everyone. I'd love to hear from you and hear how you're doing. Please drop me a note at greg@ thinkyourselfhappy.com. I'll be happy to respond to you.

The choice is all yours — and there are no limits. If you can dream it, you can have it. If you think it, you can do it. You can **Think Yourself Happy** right now, at this moment.

So get started — it's your time to develop the life of your choosing. I believe in you and wish you all the best.

Expect Great Things!

Chapter Summary

- You can change your thinking through visualization, positive anticipation, choosing your meanings, perspective, and by practicing gratitude.
- Practice these changes regularly and you'll condition your brain to create greater results.
- **Right thinking** is nothing without **follow-through.**

The Universal Success Formula is:

Right Thinking + Follow-through = Success

WHAT TO DO NEXT:

WATCH THIS VIDEO

- www.ThinkYourselfHappy.com/Chapter-9

Now That You've Finished

Find Out Your New Score:
www.TheHappinessQuiz.com

YOUR FIRST HAPPINESS SCORE

YOUR NEW HAPPINESS SCORE

10

Acknowledgments

There are many amazing people in my life who've taught, mentored, inspired, stretched, challenged, and supported me in everything I've done. My journey hasn't been my own, and the words on these pages have been written by me but were taught by masters who are far more learned and intelligent than I. But I get it and live it, and I want you to get it and live it too.

Let me start by thanking my beautiful and amazing wife Rocky, who contributes massively to my incredible life every day, as do my sons Tanner, Dillon, and Austin, whom I love, respect, and appreciate. To my mom, who's always believed in me, thank you. You're loved and appreciated more than you'll ever know. Tony Robbins, you're a man among men. You truly walk the talk and continue to passionately help others even after decades of improving the lives of tens of millions of people. I believe you're without a doubt one of the greatest teachers in the history of time, any teacher, any subject.

Thank you to my friends and the family that I've always been able to count on no matter what. I'm grateful for you every day, and you keep me grounded.

I wouldn't have it any other way. You know exactly who you are because I tell you regularly just how much I love and appreciate you. Nothing goes unsaid.

It's love that binds us, not blood. Thank you for always being honest, genuine, and having the integrity to give it to me straight every time, even when I don't like what you're telling me.

Thank you to all the people who helped and are helping me to get this message out into the world, including my editor, Victoria St. George.

Thank you to the people who make a difference, who help people, who help animals, who help make this planet a better place to be. You folks who are there for your neighbors — you're cool people!

And those of you who are genuinely happy when things go well for others — you rock, too! You're the people who inspire me to show others that happiness is there for everyone to enjoy, anytime, all the time.

You're the people I point to and talk about when I say that people in this world are good, really do care about others, and want to help. Please keep it going. Do the little things — they matter. You matter, we all matter, it all matters.

If you aren't one of these people yet, do whatever you need to do to become one of us. We're the people who are happily achieving. You're invited to join us. The water is beautiful — **jump on in!**

11

About Greg Jacobson

"Nothing is more important than feeling good about who you are, what you are doing in your life, and the people you are doing it with."
— **Greg Jacobson**

Greg lives an amazing quality of life, and teaches others how to do the same! A trusted advisor to Royalty and heads of state, mentor to experts, speakers, and authors, he is a sought-after consultant for the most respected companies and non-profits in the world. Greg volunteers his time and expertise working directly with the homeless, encarcerated, and at-risk people.

After successfully building several companies (one of them valued at over $250,000,000), he LOST IT ALL financially — including more than a dozen houses. Through it all, he figured out the secrets of how to be happy (even in a shitstorm)!

Greg teaches The 3-Keys to Living an Extraordinary Quality of Life (regardless of external circumstances). Because you can be happy, successful, and fulfilled... you just need to learn the processes.

Today, Greg combines his background in business strategies and peak performance training, with his insights on Happily Achieving to help companies dramatically improve their morale, culture, and bottom line. His proven, turnkey strategies show both employees and CEOs how to be happier and more fulfilled in their personal and professional lives, and how to create more free time to have fun with their family and friends.

Greg's mission extends throughout the world. He often speaks live at charity events, schools, and other non-profit organizations to teach personal development skills to those who have the least access to these methods and ways of thinking that are generally only available to the wealthy, high-achievers, and their families.

Greg travels to more than 20 countries and 100+ cities each year, sharing his proven techniques and wisdom learned from the great masters.

If you have ever said to yourself, "There must be more to life than this..." then Greg's techniques will change your life, fast!

12

Positive Psychology Research

Books on Happiness

Seligman, Martin E.P. *Authentic Happiness: Using the New Positive Psychology to Realize Your Potential for Lasting Fulfillment:* New York, Free Press, 200

Achor, Shawn. The Happiness Advantage: *The Seven Principles of Positive Psychology That Fuel Success and Performance at Work:* New York, Crown Business, 2010.

Ben-Shahar, Tal. Happier: *Learn the Secrets to Daily Joy and Lasting Fulfillment:* New York, McGraw-Hill Education, 2007.

Dunn, Elizabeth and Michael Norton. *Happy Money: The Science of Happier Spending:* New York, Simon & Schuster, 2013.

Emmons, Robert. *Thanks! How Practicing Gratitude Can Make You Happier:* New York, Houghton Mifflin, 2008.

Haidt, Jonathan. *The Happiness Hypothesis: Finding Modern Truth in Ancient Wisdom:* New York, Basic Books, 2005.

Klein, Stefan. *The Science of Happiness: How Our Brains Make Us Happy—and What We Can Do to Get Happier.* Translated by Stephen Lehmann. Boston, MA, Da Capo Press, 2006.

Lama, Dalai, and Dr. Howard C. Cutler. *The Art of Happiness: A Handbook for Living:* New York, Riverhead Books, 1998.

Leaf, Dr. Caroline. Switch on Your Brain: *The Key to Peak Happiness, Thinking, and Health:* Grand Rapids, MI, Baker Books, 2013.

Lyubomirsky, Sonja. *The How of Happiness: A New Approach to Getting the Life You Want:* New York, Penguin Press, 2007.McClendon III, Joseph. Get Happy Now!: Lake Dallas, TX, Success Press, 2012.

Medina, John. Brain Rules: *12 Principles for Surviving and Thriving at Work, Home, and School:* Edmonds, WA, Pear Press, 2008.

Ricard, Matthieu. Happiness: *A Guide to Developing Life's Most Important Skill:* New York, Little, Brown and Company, 2006.

Links To Studies & Statistics On Happiness

Achor, Shawn. (2011) "The Happiness Dividend." *Harvard Business Review*.
https://hbr.org/2011/06/the-happiness-dividend

Adams, Susan. (2014) "Most Americans Are Unhappy At Work." *Forbes*.
http://www.forbes.com/sites/susanadams/2014/06/20/most-americans-are-unhappy-at-work

Amabile, Teresa & Kramer, Steven. (2011) "Do Happier People Work Harder?" *New York Times*.
https://www.nytimes.com/2011/09/04/opinion/sunday/do-happier-people-work-harder.html

Kluger, Jeffrey. (2013) "The Happiness of Pursuit." *Time*.
http://content.time.com/time/magazine/article/0,9171,2146449,00.html

Morin, Amy. (2014) "7 Scientifically Proven Benefits Of Gratitude That Will Motivate You To Give Thanks Year-Round." *Forbes*.
http://www.forbes.com/sites/amymorin/2014/11/23/7-scientifically-proven-benefits-of-gratitude-that-will-motivate-you-to-give-thanks-year-round

13

NOTES

[1] Joseph McClendon III, Get Happy Now! (Lake Dallas, TX, Success Press, 2012).

[2] Jeffrey Kluger, "The Happiness of Pursuit," Time, 27 June 2013.

[3] Ibid.

[4] This list is based on the following:
❖ "…The evidence is clear: people perform better when they're happier." Amabile, Teresa & Kramer, Steven. "Employee Happiness Matters More Than You Think, Pro: Bring on the Smiles, Count the Profits," Bloomberg Business, February 2012.
https://www.london.edu/lbsr/employee-happiness-matters-more-than-you-think

❖ "…A positive mood stimulates people to be creative, tolerant, constructive, generous and non-defensive." Williams, Ray. (2015) "Slowing Down and Doing Nothing can Increase Productivity and Happiness." *Psychology Today.*
https://raywilliams.ca/slowing-down-and-doing-nothing-can-increase-productivity-and-happiness/

❖ "A worker's level of happiness has not only a profound impact on workers productivity, but also bolstered their creativity, level of commitment and improved their working relationships." Shawn Achor, "The Happiness Dividend," Harvard Business Review, 23 June 2011. *https://hbr.org/2011/06/the-happiness-dividend*

❖ "Happy people are 12% more productive at work, make better decisions, learn faster, are more optimistic, they take less unscheduled time off, they are more engaged, have less accidents, have a higher job satisfaction, are more motivated, have better physical health, have increased energy, are more pleasant to be around, and stay with a company significantly longer. In addition, the studies show that unhappy people are an additional 10% less productive. That is a 22% swing in employee productivity if they become happy." (According to Shawn Achor in The Happiness Advantage, the swing in productivity is closer to 37%.)
Oswald, Andrew J. , Proto, Eugenio & Sgroi, Daniel. (2015) "Happiness and productivity."
Journal of Labor Economics
https://wrap.warwick.ac.uk/63228/7/WRAP_Oswald_681096.pdf

[5] Marc H. Bornstein and Michael E. Lamb, Development in Infancy: An Introduction (New York: Psychology Press, 2002), n.p.

[6] Erin M. Shackell and Lionel G. Standing, "Mind Over Matter: Mental Training Increases Physical Strength," North American Journal of Psychology, 2007, Vol. 9, No. 1:189–20

[7] Brian White, "Tips from an Olympian: Visualize Your Success," San Diego Uptown News, 19 January 2013.
http://sduptownnews.com/tips-from-an-olympian-visualize-your-success

[8] Ibid.

[9] Amy Morin, "7 Scientifically Proven Benefits Of Gratitude That Will Motivate You To Give Thanks Year-Round," Forbes, 23 November 2014.
https://www.forbes.com/sites/amymorin/2014/11/23/7-scientifically-proven-benefits-of-gratitude-that-will-motivate-you-to-give-thanks-year-round

[10] Robert Emmons, Thanks! How Practicing Gratitude Can Make You Happier, (New York: Houghton Mifflin, 2008), back cover.

[11] Harvard Medical Health Center, "In Praise of Gratitude," Harvard Health Publications, 01 November 2011.
http://www.health.harvard.edu/newsletter_article/in-praise-of-gratitude

Share With Your Friends:

www.ThinkYourselfHappy.com

Want More?

Go to www.ThinkYourselfHappy.com/More

To contact Greg Jacobson about speaking, training, consulting, or mentoring go to:

www.GregJacobsonLive.com

WE ARE PRIVATELY FUNDED

PLEASE HELP US DONATE TO PEOPLE IN NEED

VISIT:
www.ThinkYourselfHappy.com/
donate-books